The Formula

The Ultimate Guide to Modern Job Finding

Pegah Gol

PASSIONPRENEUR
P U B L I S H I N G

Publishing information
Publishing, design, and production facilitated by Passionpreneur Publishing
www.PassionpreneurPublishing.com

Melbourne, VIC | Australia

To my late mother.
She always believed in me and my power of inspiration.
She never gave up on my potential and
always encouraged me to follow my dreams.
Although she is not here to applaud me anymore, I always feel her presence
and support in pursuing my goals.

And

To my father, who taught me to be adventurous in life
and to stand up stronger after each fall.

Contents

This book is divided into two parts: Preparation and Actions.

Preparation

By failing to prepare, you are preparing to fail.

—Benjamin Franklin

CHAPTER 1

The Big 'Why'

IF YOU HAVE started reading this book, then I believe that you have the motivation to start your job-hunting journey. We spend almost 30 percent of our lives at work, and nothing is more frustrating than being in an unsatisfying job every day. I will share all the steps you need to take in order to make your dream job a reality, and the first step is to identify your reasons for searching for a new job and have a clear understanding of your motivations.

Within my years of career counselling and recruitment, I have met with lots of applicants who were not fully aware of their motivations for seeking a change. So, they decided to seek out other opportunities. They applied for jobs at every opportunity without knowing why. As a result, they ended up wasting a lot of their time as well as the time of others, resulting in frustration on all sides. If you know the reason 'why', you have clarity on what kind of job opportunity, environment, organisation, and package you are targeting. These motivations then indicate which steps you need to take to achieve your objective. However, if you don't know what these reasons or motivations are, then you'll end up landing another role which is unsatisfying and frustrating. If you sought these new opportunities without understanding the real motivation of 'why', it is highly likely that you will experience the same challenges over and over again. So, I highly recommend that you find out what these underlying reasons are and ask yourself the fundamental question: 'What is my why?', because unless you know your motivations, you won't know how to move forward or what direction to move in.

If you don't know where you are going, every road will get you nowhere.

—*Henry Kissinger*

The first step is always the most crucial one despite the difficulties that come with it. Identifying the 'why' will save you time and energy and will get you the results that you are looking for. Also, it will give you a sense of direction, what to do, and even what to search for. It will provide you with a higher chance of hunting and finding a job that fulfils your needs. So it will increase your efficiency by targeting the right job.

Different people have different reasons for searching for a new job. It could be that they have been stuck in the same position for a long time and are not growing enough within the organisation. It could also be that they are underpaid for the work that they do. Perhaps they even feel weird or uncomfortable in their work environment, or they just feel unappreciated. There are loads of different elements that could be contributing to your reasons. It doesn't really matter. You need to find as many reasons as possible, then prioritise them in order of importance. This will make it easier to make a decision. If you think that you just can't find any good reason and you are just unsatisfied, it may indicate that there is something that you're unaware of. In that case, I highly recommend you see a career consultant/coach. The inquiries they make during meetings can lead you to find your 'why'. You can even ask your colleagues, family members, and recruiters for help. Sometimes, having someone looking at your situation from a different perspective can offer new insights and create a new level of awareness for you.

Many people ask me, 'So, what if I know the 'why' and it is to change my professional direction completely?' For my answer to this question, check out my next book (coming soon), which will discuss the topic of going one step further to identify your talents and find the right career option for you. Additionally, if you cannot wait until my next book is released, I conduct private career-coaching sessions for individuals in search of their true potential and those seeking the right career.

If you already know you are on the right path in your current field, and all you seek is a better job opportunity within this field, then I will be sharing some common examples of how you can do this in this chapter.

I remember one applicant whom I was helping to make a job move. He was struggling to identify his motivations. It took quite some time to find out what his reason was for seeking a change, as he was satisfied with his current company and felt that he was in the right environment and that he was earning a good salary. After going through a few possibilities together, we found that the organisation had a kind of 'flat' structure. This meant that, while it was good and fulfilling for an employee for the most part, after about a period of five years some key limitations began to emerge. The individual had reached a point where he felt, without even consciously realising it, there was no way he could improve or go any further. As a result, the only way that he felt he could grow within the organisation was if his boss moved to the next level, creating a new position for him to fill. This was his true 'why', which he wasn't aware of and which we identified in our session.

Maybe your current job requires you to work very long hours and that's leading you to lose your work–life balance. You hardly get to spend any quality time with your spouse or children, and this may cause problems in your family life. So, asking your family about this can help you detect these issues that you may not even be aware of. Therefore, your work–life balance becomes your 'why' for seeking a change.

In case you are still unsure about your 'whys', here are some common points to help you identify them:

1) You are looking for new challenges at work.
2) Your company is restructuring.
3) Your job duties have been reduced.
4) Your company underwent a merger or an acquisition.
5) You are not getting enough recognition at work from your management.
6) Your company's growth prospects are poor.
7) Your boss did not keep his promises (of a promotion or a raise, for instance).
8) Your job became boring, and you grew sick of it.
9) You don't want to work overtime.
10) You have to travel on business too often.
11) You are to be sent to a faraway foreign location.
12) You need to be able to take better care of your family (work–life balance).

13) You are looking for better career prospects, professional growth, and job opportunities.
14) You are employed for one project or on a short-term contract and are looking for a permanent position.

After sharing these examples above, I'm going to share with you some tips that can enable you to identify your motivations.

First things first. Just sit in a quiet place and think about your 'whys'. Have a pen and paper ready and begin to write down whatever comes to mind. The most important thing at this stage is to be honest with yourself. Write as many reasons as you can. In fact, it would be better to have more than one reason and make sure to write all of them down. Prioritise them one by one while considering their level of importance. Figure out the one troubling you the most, thereby egging you on to make your next move. I believe that your job package and income have less of an effect on your job satisfaction, even if it still is an important factor. If you enjoy your role and your organisational environment, the financial side will naturally fall into place. Regardless, don't be shy about including this as one of your reasons.

If you cannot find what exactly is motivating you to want to move, then find the most irritating or unsatisfying factor in your current job. Something that hampers you from waking up in the morning with a burning desire to go to work.

Sometimes, life runs away from you and increasing financial responsibilities put you in a situation where you don't look too deeply to find the reasons behind what is making you unsatisfied or unhappy in your current job. Remember that you don't want to spend 30 percent of your life in a frustratingly unsatisfying job. So, taking a breather and thinking deeply about your reasons is a basic but crucial step to find direction in your next job move. Consider anything that makes you think about moving to another job.

To summarise this chapter, here are three actions you can take to start you on your journey:

1) You need to know your 'whys'. Understand the reason or reasons *why* you're looking for a different opportunity, and make sure you're being sincere.
2) The best way to keep track of your reasons and motivations is to write them down and prioritise them in order and find the most important or frustrating one.
3) Ask other people to help you to find your reasons. Asking your family members, your colleagues, or your career coach can help you to identify your motivations.

Now that you've found your 'whys', it's time to move on to the next chapter.

Chapter 2

Your Job-Hunting Fuel

After you find your motivation and 'whys', you should be aware of the challenges you will face in your job-hunting journey. It is crucial to keep being persistent in your search.

Just as cars don't move without fuel, your search would go nowhere without your fuel. Your desire keeps you positive, even if the situation may not be promising. The energy that you put in will come back to you and will increase your efficiency. We will go through the challenges that you may face and the ways to overcome these challenges in this chapter.

In my years of recruitment and headhunting experience, I've come across many applicants who didn't get disappointed with rejection and were always available and keen to pursue all kinds of opportunities. They always landed on the next, better prospect. Those who keep their fuel levels high will get not only one opportunity but, in fact, multiple ones to freely choose from. Your fuel is what gets you running. Without it, you could get depressed, frustrated, and exhausted, or you could experience any other negative feelings which will not serve you in your search.

You've done it before and you can do it now. See the positive
possibilities. Redirect the substantial energy of your frustration
and turn it into positive, effective, unstoppable determination.

—Ralph Marston

Opportunities arise from time to time, so don't expect to get notified if you are not being smart with your search. Keep your fuel levels high, accept that you may face disappointments, but know that, with persistence, you will eventually find those golden opportunities when the time comes. The best thing to do is to be consistent in your job search. Don't get disappointed with rejection. Sometimes it's better to lose this one to make way for an even better opportunity.

Expectation Management
Recruitment comes under the area of the human resources department, and there is a very valid reason for this: it involves humans making decisions. They look for factors such as capability and competency in the applicants, but there are also other factors to look out for, such as matching the applicant's personality with the organisation and the team. Imagine how many people are applying for the same job that you've applied for. The processes of getting your CV recognised and the interviews which come after are lengthy, so just be realistic with your expectations and, at the same time, put your eggs in different baskets (apply for as many relevant jobs as you can) to avoid frustration and disappointment.

I remember a candidate who was looking for new opportunities, and at his level of expertise, which was quite high, the movement in the market was very slow. We struggled to find him a job even though I knew how experienced he was. He always kept up a warm connection with me, calling to check from time to time if there were any suitable opportunities for him. After almost eight months, when I had completely forgotten about his profile, he called up again, and I was looking for someone with similar experience, and boom! He landed up with the perfect job just by being consistent in his search.

Channels

Check all the channels, that is, LinkedIn, job boards, CV banks, marketing boards, etc., to avoid missing out on opportunities. Remember that there are some hidden opportunities that won't be shared anywhere as they are sensitive or confidential. Therefore, being in touch with a couple of recruiting agencies gives you a higher chance of employment. Keep searching; keep your fuel levels high.

Network

Make sure your network grows. Start with people whom you know, and let them know that you are in search of a new job. Attend workshops, meetups, and seminars. Register with different groups on LinkedIn. Get in touch with hiring managers, and ask them for recommendations. Networking by far increases your chances of getting job opportunities.

Positivity

Make sure you stay positive while you are searching. Your fuel levels could be depleted by many factors, and it is important not to let this happen. There are long periods of silence, rejections in the process, jobs being put on hold, or organisations going through a hiring freeze or structural changes. Whatever happens during your job-hunting process, stay positive and be patient. I recommend reading inspirational books on how to stay positive, or biographies of successful people, in an effort to keep your fuel levels high.

You may be asking yourself, 'What if I keep doing all this and still nothing happens?'

I would say, keep your fuel levels high and, along with the other tips in the rest of this book, you will learn smarter ways to keep your chances high as well. There might be some jobs that you are unaware of. What if, when you just gave up, some opportunities came by? I am sure you don't want to miss that just because you got disappointed and allowed your fuel to get depleted.

How Long Should I Keep Searching?

There are certain factors on which your job search depends. Your seniority is a big factor. On the one hand, if you are a senior at C level, it might take longer. On the other hand, more fast-paced jobs make your search easier. For example, if you are in sales, your role is in demand; if the movement in the market is high, the possibility of you getting more opportunities is also high. The timeline depends on your situation. Try to be realistic with your timeline, and you will surely find a suitable opportunity.

What If the Market Is Not Good and Opportunities Are Not There?

Even in the worst market, there will always be someone leaving their job, someone moving out of the country, someone moving to a better opportunity, or someone getting promoted; so there is always the possibility of a vacancy. All you need to do is to keep your fuel levels high and keep searching.

To summarise this chapter:

1) Manage your expectations: Just by applying for the first job does not mean you will land that role successfully. Recruitment and job searches are lengthy processes that involve going through the recruitment and selection funnel as well as personality matches. Be persistent with your search; know what you are aiming to get; and eventually, you will land your targeted role.

2) Put your eggs in different baskets: Apply for many relevant jobs. Avoid submitting your profile for one job and then just waiting around for that response. The higher the number of jobs you apply for, the higher the possibility of landing a relevant role successfully.

3) No disappointment: There may be rejections in your search, and it is a part of the process. Keep yourself positive by, for example, reading inspirational books about successful people. What these books taught me was to understand that it was not easy for anyone. Ensure that you're checking all the resources often so you can get prompt notifications of relevant job opportunities.

I shall be sharing more tips and tricks in the coming chapters. By the time you finish reading this book, you will have very practical tools to help you find a suitable opportunity successfully.

CHAPTER 3

Top Secrets

WHAT ARE THE Top Secrets of the Job-Searching and Job-Finding Industries?

There are some secret steps that recruiters know. Hiring managers are also aware of them, but the candidates who are applying for the jobs don't know about these steps. This is a very important part of your job search, and you need to know about these tips and tricks. The most important thing is not to use these tips unless you're sure that you are really a good fit for the opportunity. This is very important because, if you use these tips and apply them to a job that does not really match with your profile, it will have a negative effect on your application and reputation.

Why is it important to know all these secrets? These secrets save you time and energy, and you will also get the results much faster than the normal way of doing things. As you know, it's always good to have shortcuts, and these secrets are your shortcuts to reach that desired job.

In my experience, almost 90 percent of job applicants don't know about these secrets. I will share with you how to increase your chances of getting positive results from your search in this chapter.

Most Jobs Don't Get Advertised

When vacancies arise within an organisation, either through the expansion of the business, or vacation, resignation or promotion of the job holder, organisations look for someone internally. It would be fair to all existing employees to get the chance first. They post the job internally or ask the existing hiring manager if they know of anyone suitable in their team. That doesn't mean they would say no if someone external shows interest to join the organisation at just the right time. You can find leads through the movements and strategies of organisations within the market. By being aware of these different organisational movements, you could be the right candidate at the right moment.

Almost 30 percent of new hiring happens through referrals. In case the internal process is not successful, hiring managers ask around in their network for referrals. Here is where your network links in with your net worth. Always keep your network updated regarding your job search. If you are planning to move, they should know first.

Hot Leads

Either hot leads or no chance at all. Hot leads are vacancies that are posted or advertised for two weeks to a maximum of a month. It's very likely that the employer will find the ideal candidates in the initial stage, and, if the time has expired, it is unlikely that they would search for more. It is the perfect time to send in an application for a position. Always check the date of advertisement for the role. If, for example, it is from two months ago, it is likely that the position has already been filled and the organisation has forgotten to remove the advertisement. An exception could be that the role is super technical and rare in the market.

There was an applicant who, every time, used to call us after a job post expired, asking if she could still apply for it! Obviously, the selection would be made by that time, so I suggested that she create a notification for her targeted job. Having followed that protocol and after applying a few times, she finally got selected for an interview.

Importance of Hiring Managers

Internal recruiters are your key contacts, but initially, you don't need to apply for a job only through the people in the human resources department. This secret is very important and should not be a common practice. If you see a role being posted by an internal recruiter, you can always find the relevant hiring manager of that role and see if they are within your network. Ask them if they think your profile is suitable enough for the role and suggest that they recommend you to the recruitment department. You need to keep in mind that it is not the hiring manager's job to hire you directly. Respect the process by only asking them as a favour, and avoid contacting them if they are not within your network.

Recruitment Agencies

Any recruitment service companies, from executive search firms to recruitment companies and outplacement firms, consider you as an asset. They are the most active people in the search for candidates. At the same time, they have a very high-volume list of vacancies, and they need to deliver at least three candidates per vacancy. They are the best source for you, so if you can build rapport with them, you have a higher chance of receiving a call every time a relevant vacancy comes up.

There were a few candidates who built a very good rapport with the team, and every time we had certain jobs, we always remembered their names and got in touch with them. They all landed these new opportunities successfully, as they kept their relationships with us close and professional.

'What if my network is not big enough and I don't have many hiring managers or recruiters in my network?' Then I highly recommend that you start working on your network strategy and make your network bigger. If you don't know how to do this, I will be covering it in Chapter 5. You can also attend my networking workshops. In these workshops, you can expect to learn the ways of networking. You also have a chance to network with different people and start your network expansion process.

What if the job is in a very specific niche and the job is still available after a month? Unless the role is very rare or technical, the possibility of it still being available (still in the selection process) after this long is very low. It depends on your role. If it meets these criteria, you could ask your recruiter or call the organisation and ask whether it is still available.

To summarise this chapter:

1) Always be on the search for new job posts. Look at the job posting dates. Look at websites and LinkedIn to see if the date on which the job was posted is less than two weeks

ago. Create a notification for the job to get notifications by email or on LinkedIn. This is very easy nowadays, as most jobs are posted online.

2) Make sure you get insider information via your network—ask those in your industry what is happening in the current organisation. Become a great networker, stay connected, expand your network by attending seminars, and use the tips provided in Chapter 5.

3) Ask recruiters for certain jobs, look at the job boards of recruitment agencies, or pick up the phone and get information from relevant recruiters. They will tell you if a job is still available, as sometimes it gets shortlisted in less than five days.

CHAPTER 4

No More Old-Fashioned

DO YOU REMEMBER the time that you sent your CV by fax or you applied for a job with the hard copy of your CV and got the job? Those times are what I call old-fashioned. We are already twenty years into the twenty-first century, and as technology is growing so fast, job-searching trends and employment techniques have improved big time.

What Would Be the Benefits of Learning How Not to Be Old-Fashioned?
It will show your credibility, and it will increase the chances of being noticed. Recruiters are also up to date with new ways of sourcing and update themselves faster with market knowledge. Technology has grown fast, and it is time for you to grow faster.

The fact is, approaching it the old-fashioned way will mean you will miss the future train which has tremendous possibilities. You'll end up staying where you are at the moment and missing opportunities, thereby staying behind and getting frustrated.

Being up to date with new ways of applying will increase your chances of being noticed and will show your credibility to your next employer. That is, increasing your chances of being noticed is equal to increasing your chances of getting the interview.

For that, you need to update yourself by using new technology to grow your knowledge in new ways. Ask recruiters and members of your network and find out how they apply. Leave the old-fashioned ways where they belong and learn about new tools. Use platforms like LinkedIn and other new technological ways such as soft-copy CV, job boards, CV bank websites and recruitment agencies.

> *Despite our high rate of unemployment, 300,000 jobs go unfilled largely because many of the unemployed lack the skills needed today as a result of technological progress.*
>
> *—Kim Campbell*

Soft-Copy CV

Your CV needs to be in a soft-copy format, such as a Word document or PDF. My advice for creating your soft-copy CV is to go with Word documents, as it will increase your chances of being found in most of job search engines. Nowadays most recruiters and employers use a type of software called ATS, short for "applicant tracking system", during the hiring process to collect, sort, scan, and rank the job applications they receive for their open positions. Your Word-document version soft-copy formatted CV is more ATS friendly, and it allows the software to find the relevant keywords on your CV easily. Remember the keywords in your CV are the 'keys' which allow you to be found in most of the search engines of job boards.

CV Bank Websites

Any website where you can register and submit your CV to be found by future employers is called a CV bank. After submitting your CV and conforming to certain criteria, you will be in their database; and when future employers run a search on their CV bank to find relevant profiles, if your CV is optimised and has the relevant keywords, then it will easily appear in their search. There are plenty of them in every part of the world, and you need to find the local, most used ones to get higher chances of appearing in a recruiter's or employer's search. I suggest that if you are not actively looking for another opportunity, don't submit your profile to all CV banks or job boards as it may appear in your current employer's search as well and create the impression that you are looking to move actively. Even in this situation, there are options that allow you to protect your data or just keep your profile anonymous.

Job Boards

There are websites that only post jobs directly through employers, and when you search for certain jobs, you could end up getting a list of the same jobs but with different employers. When you apply, you will directly submit to those particular employers' databases. In case you want to protect your profile and you are not so active with your search, I suggest this method as a much better way to apply when compared to CV banks.

Recruitment Agencies

These companies only advertise active jobs, and they remove the job ad as soon as the position gets filled. Recruiters are efficient with their CV searches, as relevant CVs would be assets to them. Thus, it would be easier for you to follow up with them, but only if you believe you are right for the role. After submitting your CV, you should wait for a few days and then call the agency directly and speak to the recruitment agent who posted the job ad.

LinkedIn

LinkedIn is a powerful tool that could dramatically increase your chances of being seen by prospective employers. LinkedIn is a social media platform used by those seriously seeking new jobs, so remember to keep it professional. It's the perfect tool for networking in a professional way. Why do I keep emphasising the professionalism of this platform? Because it's unlike other social media platforms that are mainly used for finding friends. If you are looking for normal networking and new or old friends, there are other social media platforms that you can use. LinkedIn is more formal and is used as an opportunity for networking. It's a social platform used for job searches by job seekers and companies who are in search of potential employees like you. Representing yourself on LinkedIn nowadays is very normal, unlike being on job boards; and being active is not a sign of desperation. On the contrary, it is a sign of acting professional, knowing your worth, and representing yourself in the best way possible.

What if you don't have access to technology, or you are unfamiliar with the different tools mentioned above? We are actually in a technological era. You should use it to help yourself in your new job search. You can start by asking people you know and trust to help you learn how to use these technologies. However, the way in which you ask people is key. Show your enthusiasm and your gratitude, and I guarantee that they won't mind helping you. However, what if, when you've just finished learning how to use a new technology, you reach the point where there are new trends, new ways to do it? Well, learn the new ways. Keep updating yourself to reach where you need to be so that you are moving at the same speed as your industry.

The best thing to do is to make sure that you update yourself with all the new tools and technologies related to job searching. Make sure that you ask the people you know and trust to help you with this part of your journey. Ask them how they got their jobs and how they had a successful interview. Also, use LinkedIn. It is the best tool and the most modern way of being noticed and of getting your CV out there. You can also always use the help of professionals.

Since being up to date with technology is essential for all of us, I run regular workshops regarding all the technologies mentioned above to make sure that you are all set and up to date with your technological job searches.

To summarise this chapter:

1) Create a search-friendly soft-copy CV in the form of a Word document, using loads of relevant keywords. In Chapter 6 of this book, you will find some essential tips on how to build a strong CV.

2) Register your profile with major CV banks within your current area or your targeted area. Also, submit your CV online with job boards, recruitment agencies, or LinkedIn to increase your chances of getting noticed.

3) If you think you need help getting up to date with new technological trends, ask someone in your network for help. Alternatively, you can book a free consultation appointment with me to check which areas we need to focus on so we can work together to increase your online appearance.

CHAPTER 5

Be a Superhero

I'M SURE YOU'RE familiar with the word 'superhero'. Superheroes are people with some sort of superpower and a willingness to help people when they're in need. You may be wondering why this chapter is called 'Be a Superhero' while we are talking about networking.

Your superhero power is your willingness to help others, so while you search for your own job, you can also be helpful to others. This is your superpower which will make you popular and push you in the right direction.

It is literally true that you can succeed best and quickest by helping others to succeed.

—Napoleon Hill

Why Is It Necessary to Be a Superhero?
By helping other job-seekers, you make yourself memorable. People usually remember those who have helped them, and you also get a good feeling when you help someone achieve something; so it brings lots of positivity into your life. Also, by this small gesture of helping, your network is going to go one step further, because by helping other people and by referring them to jobholders, your

image in the eyes of those you help will change the perceptions of all members within your network and everyone will come to notice you as a helpful person. As a result, these people will prefer to interview you if suitable opportunities come up. They will basically, favour you over the other people who they do not see superheroes. It will also increase your chances of receiving help from them when you need it.

But first, you need to have a solid network, and networking should be an ongoing strategy. A higher percentage of jobs get filled through networking. In today's job scenario, it is crucial to have a proper network strategy. There are certain concerns regarding the topic of networking that will affect your networking efficiency.

We will go through a few of them here:

1) I am not good at networking; I am shy.
2) People think I just want to get a job.
3) I may disturb them.
4) It doesn't feel right to get in touch with old colleagues.

For some of these concerns, like shyness, there are some techniques that you can practise. I offer these techniques in my workshops. For the other concerns, the fact is, people like to be helpful, and they will happily share information. They enjoy talking about their experiences. If you recognise their greatness and are willing to help them as well, you will be considered a superhero among them.

Just imagine what will happen if you're not willing to help and you're just receiving help from others. Usually, people who are not willing to help others become isolated; they feel lonely and left out, and the chance of them getting referred for a job or getting any help from their network automatically decreases. We don't want to get to that point. What is the best thing to do? Just be there for others and volunteer any help that you can. The help that you can provide to people is not always financial, and you can start to refer job-seekers to other organisations when they post job applications. Even if they don't make it in the selection process, you are still helping them. You can always find a way to help people, and by doing this, you achieve a higher rank of popularity.

In the recruitment and job-searching industry, it's always recommended to be a superhero by using referrals as a good tool to do whatever you can for other job-seekers. You can start referring applicants to your recruiters who you think are relevant for certain jobs. You can also keep yourself up to date with job opportunities and update other job-seekers with any vacancies that are suitable for them. Also, by helping the recruiters, it only helps you to improve your own chances. Even recruiters will be more willing to help you in return!

The best thing to do is to start helping your network by volunteering to share suitable vacancies with them, referring other job-seekers to jobholders, helping them with CV writing, providing them with any help in learning how to apply for a job, helping them with their interview preparation, or providing them with information on the culture of the organisation they're looking to apply to. I'm sure that, by reading this book, you're going to get lots of practical tips on how to help others to get their dream jobs and find better opportunities. Another thing you could do to help others in their job search is to recommend that they read this book so they have the same opportunities as you do to learn these practical job-search tips and tricks. Just make sure that you don't forget to think of yourself in the process! Try to find an opportunity for yourself first. These are the keys to a much higher chance of getting help in return.

I remember one particular candidate who was, in fact, my inspiration for writing this chapter. He was one of my favourite candidates, and he left some marks on my life that will never let me forget him. How? He was just unstoppable in helping others by not only referring people to me but also to job opportunities that might be right for them. He always called me and updated me about new job opportunities that arose, and I'm sure he was doing this for other people as well. By helping me, he made me set out on the mission to help him. I went out of my way to help him find better opportunities, though I wasn't actually obliged to do so. I willingly wanted to go out of my way to do this for him. So, I ended up placing him in a better job, and in all these years that I've known him, not only did I help him land a better opportunity, but he also helped three other people from his network find better job opportunities by referring them to me for jobs that I had posted and which were suitable for them. In this way, he constantly grew in his career.

This was the best example of a superhero for me. I called him a superhero, and the whole concept of 'superhero' came from this particular candidate because it was just what he was. He was a superhero in the recruitment industry, in his industry, and within his network.

I cannot emphasise more on how important it can be to be a super-hero for others.

What if, even though you help everyone you can, you don't seem to receive anything in return? I am sure you are familiar with the first law of energy. This law states that every drop of energy that you put into helping others will, in the process, come back to you. It might not come back to you from the same person, but one way or another, you will see the result.

Always have faith that, somehow, things will turn out in your favour.

You may wonder, 'What if people don't want me to refer them to a recruiter, or what if they're not currently looking for a job?' In my ten years of experience in recruitment, I have never had a single situation where, if someone referred another person to me and I called the other person, they reacted to it negatively or with surprise. This is because people naturally appreciate and welcome new and better opportunities, even if they aren't actively seeking a change in their job. In fact, they normally ask who referred them so they can thank that person for their help.

However, you always have the option to ask that person and get their permission if you feel like they may not be comfortable with you sharing their contact and other personal details. You could ask them directly whether they would like you to refer them. In this case, you're doing it with no guilt and they will remember the gesture, and if something comes up, they will be willing to refer you to other people in turn.

To summarise this chapter, here are a few ways in which you can be a superhero:

1) Willingness: Just be willing to volunteer whatever you can for people when they are looking for a better opportunity. Ask them what you can do for them, even if they don't ask for help. This will create the impression of you being helpful in their minds, and, in return, they will remember you if there are opportunities that they can help you with. You can refer them to read this book so they can use the tips I've included here to find better job opportunities much more efficiently.

2) Job recommendation: If you come across any role which you think might be suitable for anyone in your network during your job search, recommend it to them without any hesitation. This will help them remember you if they find any job opportunity within their search or within their networks that might suit you.

3) Referring: Use referral as a tool to help other people and your organisation. And, if you choose to attend my counselling sessions and you find them suitable, which I hope you do, you can refer me to other people within your network so they can attend my workshops as well.

Remember, it is always a good feeling to be a superhero, and helping others always has its own rewards.

CHAPTER 6

You Are Your CV

I AM QUITE sure that, if you are working or have worked in the past, you have at least one CV for your entire career to date. If you don't have one, then I highly recommend that you start creating one.

What Is a CV?

CV is short for 'curriculum vitae', and it is the first requirement when applying for a job. It's a powerful document that shows your qualifications, professional experience, abilities, and achievements. It speaks on your behalf, and ultimately it should highlight why you're the best person for the job.

Your CV is a summary of you on paper. So, how should your CV look? First, ask yourself these questions. How do you prepare for an interview? Do you wear a professional outfit? Do you look smart and polished? Think of your CV as a representation of you ready for your interview. Now, imagine your CV gets to its destination before you do, which is normally how it happens. If it's not so impressive, it doesn't have the effect that you're looking for, and it may end up in the bin.

If you want some tips to write your CV, I am sure you can find CV writing books with lots of techniques. But, what I am trying to discuss here is something you may not find in those books. I am here to make the point that your CV should represent you in your entirety.

In my career as a recruiter, I have seen many CVs from fresh graduates to senior executives, and I can clearly differentiate between the CVs that were written by third parties and the CVs that got my attention because they were unique. I am not referring to those colourful or odd-looking CVs, but to those that were outstanding for a different reason and which were not clichéd. I am a big fan of writing your own CV. Try to avoid giving it to third parties because it may result in you receiving a cold and repetitive CV. There is no harm in getting a professional to help you write your CV, but giving the whole process of creating your CV to an organisation is a mistake. I explain why below.

Let me give you a real example of some workshops that I have done for fresh finance graduates on their career day. I asked them, 'So, you put the major you've studied and your university plus maybe some internship that you've done on your CV. Do you think that is what makes you different from the whole lot of graduates who have studied the same subject?' So, the question is, what makes you different from the rest? The answer is what else you put in there. What makes you outstanding for the job you are applying for? We all have some unique qualities in our personality that will aid us in landing that perfect job. The question you should ask yourself is, what is that unique quality? So, before you start writing your CV, you need to understand what job you are targeting and then take the time to ask yourself what your unique qualities are. Put time into your CV. Make your CV worthwhile by turning it into something that becomes a reflection of yourself and what you stand for.

I suggest that, before you read the rest of this chapter, take a while and think deeply about these two points.

Most careers start with a CV. The CV is the most important step of your job search, and it needs to be written well, in the best and most professional way; it should be crafted for the role you are applying for. Let's discuss why.

As I mentioned earlier, your CV will work on your behalf. You don't need to personally apply for every single job opportunity. You can easily, with just one click, send your CV, and it does the trick for you. It saves lots of time for you and does lots of things on your behalf.

Before I start writing about how your CV should look, I would like to mention something very important; it may seem very clichéd and old-fashioned but, especially in earlier days, it was a necessity: the cover letter. A cover letter was a very important tool back in those days when you submitted your printed CV in order to protect your confidential personal information. Nowadays, however, many submissions are made via email, thus making a cover letter something extra and without much of a purpose. Instead, you can type a summary of your profile in the email itself so as to draw the attention of the interviewer to your CV quickly. So, unless you submit a hard copy of your CV in person, avoid attaching a cover letter as an extra soft-copy document along with your CV so you can promote your CV in the proper way.

If your summary is reasonable and professional, it will convince the hiring manager, within just a couple of minutes, to open your attached CV and to request to meet you face-to-face. Obviously, it will also increase the chances of you getting the interview.

You can put all of your achievements, both professional and personal, in just this one section.

I know lots of job-seekers who lose the chance of getting an interview in a job search by submitting a CV that is confusing or not written well. They end up not being selected for the interview. At the end of the day, they feel left out and wonder why they're not being noticed. They feel that the whole process of recruitment or the job search is not working well. They don't understand that it's all because they don't have an impressive CV.

So, what is an impressive CV? It's a well-written, professional CV. It should be easy to read and should have a collection of your experiences, qualifications, and achievements. Your achievements are especially important and need to be emphasised, so don't be shy to share all your details and credentials.

The question is how you can put all this information in just one or two pages maximum. I'm going to give you a few tips on what is best for the most professional CV.

The first thing that I can say is to just keep it short. Your CV is not a book, and it's not an essay, either. It's a summary of your professional experience and qualifications. Most of the employers and professionals in human resource departments don't have time to go through lengthy CVs covering five to six pages just to understand what you have done fifteen years ago when you were doing an internship. Things that go back quite some time may not be as important as something recent. For example, if you have just graduated and have done an internship, it would be very important to include this information in your CV. However, if you're a very senior person in your field and you have more than fifteen to twenty years of experience, having your internship experience in your CV is just not going to be very impressive. I suggest that, after a few years, try to emphasise only the most recent parts of your CV.

Another thing that I always see in so many candidates when they are applying for different jobs is that they have confusing CVs. They apply for a certain job, but I'm often not sure if that candidate is right for the role or not. There are lots of heavy words, and the subject matter is confusing. It is always better to avoid any heavy or negative words or any kind of confusion. Just keep your CV very short and very well-written.

I remember one of my friends who asked me for help with her CV. When she sent it to me, I was not sure what to do. She's a close friend, and I am well aware of what she'd been doing, but by reading her CV that information was absolutely unclear. If I didn't know her, I don't think I would have understood what she does professionally. This blocked her chances of getting any interviews. So, when we worked on a new CV, we made her responsibilities crystal clear, and soon she got much better opportunities.

Another point that I can really emphasise is that you should always write the truth. Mentioning the truth and being honest about what you've done is the key, and this will be proven in the process. You might get away with having your CV being really impressive, but then, in the interview, the opposite shows through. And, even if you pass the interview, at work you're going to have the truth come out, and you'll be stuck. It's definitely not a situation that you want to be in.

Avoid exaggerating something that you've done. It's nice to show off and it's nice to mention your achievements, but if it's something that's part of a daily routine job, it is completely needless and baseless to highlight it.

I'm sure that, by now, you might start to question your CV and think, 'Is my CV representing me in the right way or not?' If you don't know how to write your CV, the best thing to do is to get an expert to help you write your CV along with you. Alternatively, you can come to some of the workshops that I offer and learn how to do it yourself. We can even do it on your behalf with the information that you provide us with.

It is necessary to have a well-written, professional CV. But how would you know if your CV is well-written and professional enough? You can ask your network. You can ask recruiters if you've built rapport with them. You can show your CV to other job-seekers or those who are already working around you and just ask them what they think. This is exactly what my friend did, and that is how I was able to mention to her that this was not the right CV for her. I'm sure that when people look at your CV, they're not going to just say that it's all right, that it's nice. They're going to ask you what you're doing. Or, they're going to say that they understand what you're doing. The best thing to do is just ask people's opinions, always.

It is important to bear in mind that no one gets a job just because their CV is exceptional and well written, of course. Even though the CV is the most important part of the process, it's not all of the process, but it certainly will get the attention of the interviewer. So, as long as you have a CV that represents you well along with the rest of the tips and techniques that I give you in the other chapters of this book, you will have the formula in your hand to increase the possibilities of you getting a suitable job.

These are the sections you should include in your CV:

1) Name, professional title, and contact details
2) Summary of your professional profile of experiences
3) Experience, employment history, and a description of each role
4) Education and qualifications
5) Key skills and competencies
6) Hobbies, interests, and references

Here are some formatting and spacing guidelines to keep in mind when building your CV:

1) Length: Keep it short. Your CV is not your biography; it should be a summary of your experience, achievements and credentials
2) Font type and size: Make sure you are using the same font and size throughout your CV. Use the most professional and proper size font.
3) Page margins and tailoring: The CV should look coherent; use the same margins and tailoring in all pages to make it easy to read for the hiring managers
4) Keywords and ATSs: Increase the chances of being tracked and found by the search engines and recruiters by

using many relevant keywords to the role you are applying. Keywords in your CV are the 'keys' which make your CV match to the relevant vacancy.

5) Saving the file: use the most up-to-date version of the software that you use for saving soft-copy formatted CV, as the CV may appear differently if it is saved with an outdated software.

Don't forget that your CV is a very important part of your career. So, to summarise this chapter:

1) Put time into writing your CV. Keep it short and well written. Avoid any kind of negative words. Get help from professionals, but don't put the entire process in their hands. Always write the truth.

2) You are your CV, so show the pride you have in yourself in your CV. Don't be shy to mention your career achievements. Your achievements are what make your job description unique; otherwise, your CV is going to be 'just another job description'.

3) Your CV should highlight what you've done differently, what you've done best, and how you've achieved these things. One look at your CV should make a person think, 'I should meet that candidate.'

Actions

The path to success is to take massive, determined actions.

—Tony Robbins

CHAPTER 7

Master the Interview

CONGRATULATIONS, YOU HAVE managed to pass through the difficult part, which is getting your powerful CV to put you in front of the interviewers and make them interested to meet you. Now what?

The interview is the stage of decision-making for hiring managers. It is the point where they're not only going to see and understand your work experience, but they will also understand your personality and check whether you are the best fit for the role and for the organisation. Before this stage, it was just your CV doing the work for you, and the hiring managers could see on paper whatever you'd written. Now is the time for action by proving to them, in person, why they should believe you are the most suitable candidate for the position.

The shocking truth is that several job searches stop at this stage, and it is definitely not due to a lack of experience. It is mostly because of a lack of interview skills and preparation when showing up to the interview. So, it's important to show up completely prepared for the interview. Interview preparation and techniques are both equally important. Let's discuss why they are so important. Being well prepared will get you a better chance of getting the job, and it will help you to be more confident in the interview. If you're prepared for the interview, your confidence will come naturally, and this helps in the flow of the interview process. You'll avoid embarrassment and disappointment. Preparation, in a way, also guarantees your success.

> *Give me six hours to chop down a tree and I will spend the*
> *first four sharpening the axe.*

> —*Abraham Lincoln*

By being prepared well for your interview, you are sharpening your axe; then the interview will only be a bridge for you to your next job opportunity.

So, what are the methods and techniques you should use to prepare for your interview?

There are certain steps you need to pass through before you appear for your interview:

1) Do some research about the organisation and the interviewer/s.
2) Understand the job description well.
3) Prepare yourself for the most common interview questions.
4) Be well aware and ready for questions related to all of your achievements.
5) Make yourself aware of the culture and dress code of the organisation.
6) Prepare yourself to be there ahead of time.
7) If it is required for you to do a presentation, be well prepared for it.
8) Make a list of possible questions that you would like to ask if they are not covered during the interview

Why do we need to practise the interview and be prepared? First of all, it will help you to understand the people you're going to meet beforehand so you can build rapport with them. It will help you to be prepared to talk about your achievements and to answer certain clichéd questions that you're going to be asked. This will increase your credibility. So, before you show up for the interview, you are already prepared for more than 50 percent of what is required to achieve success in the process.

Personality Preparation
Building initial rapport with the interviewers is a part of personality preparation, and here is why you should try to do research about the personality of the interviewers. It takes people only seven seconds to make a judgement about others, and during that time, the interviewer/s make crucial determinations about you, including your likeability, your personality, and how well you would fit in with organisation culture and others on the team.

How would you know how to prepare yourself to meet some people whom you have never met before? There are certain ways you can begin to practise for the interview. These include using LinkedIn to check their profiles, using certain job boards, searching for their profiles, searching on the Internet for some press news about them, and possibly even finding some people inside the organisation and asking them about the personality of the interviewer/s.

Common Interview Questions Preparation
After the personality research and preparation, start preparing to answer some basic questions about yourself. Consider this list as your interview question study guide.

1) Can you tell me a little about yourself?
2) What makes you unique?
3) Why do you want to work here?
4) What interests you about this role?
5) What motivates you?
6) What are you passionate about?
7) Why are you leaving your current job?
8) What are your greatest strengths?
9) What are your greatest weaknesses?
10) What are your goals for the future?
11) Where do you see yourself in five years?
12) Why should we hire you?
13) What is your salary range expectation?
14) What did you like most about your last position?
15) What did you like least about your last position?
16) How do you deal with pressure or stressful situations?
17) What type of work environment do you prefer?
18) What is your greatest accomplishment?
19) Can you tell us about a difficult work situation and how you overcame it?
20) How would your boss and co-workers describe you?

List of Your Achievements

It is equally important to prepare for the interview in terms of the job description and organisation you are applying to and to prepare yourself by memorising all your achievements.

Let's assume that you show up for the interview on time, dressed smartly; you are well prepared to be asked certain questions relevant to the job that you're applying for because you've read through and understood the job description prior to the interview. Now, imagine if they ask you about your achievements and you just don't remember them. You know what you've achieved, but because you didn't prepare yourself, you cannot really elaborate on them and you don't have the facts and figures that would show them how much you have achieved. So to avoid any embarrassment, make sure you have all the answers prior to your interview.

I remember one of the candidates I was interviewing for a position on my team. He amazed me because he was super, super ready for the interview. Whatever I asked, I knew that he already had the answer ready. There were even certain questions that were very specifically set for the job that he had applied for. One thing that made me very keen to recruit this person was that he had a list of his achievements ready and explained how he achieved them. It is equally important to prepare your list of achievements and to prepare to explain how you achieved each one accordingly.

Ask Relevant Questions

Following this, make sure you have a list of possible questions that you would like to ask if they are not covered during the interview.

'What if the interviewer or interviewers are not friendly? They didn't let me talk or ask anything.' You may also feel that all your preparation has gone to waste. In this case, there could be two possibilities: either you did not prepare yourself specifically for this interview, or sometimes certain situations may not be as ideal as you had predicted. Normally, in this situation, it's best to just stay confident, be natural, and go with the flow of the interview. By just being prepared, you already boost your confidence, and the rest will fall into place naturally. You'll always have a chance to send an email after the interview to ask your questions.

Flexibility

You may encounter this kind of situation with an organisation. They may not have a specific job description in mind, or they may be flexible on the matter, meaning they may create a suitable profile for each applicant.

There was another situation where we had an internal vacancy due to the expansion of our company, but we had no specific role in mind. We did not share any specific job description with candidates, because there were a variety of jobs that we were recruiting for and we were quite flexible on the matter. We started to meet with a few of the shortlisted candidates, and the one who actually got our attention was the one who asked specific questions about specific scenarios. This indicated how ready she was, even if we were to speak about various roles relevant to her experience. We did not ask our questions about specific roles; neither did we discuss different job opportunities. Her questions made us happy with her flexibility and in-depth knowledge of the industry, and we were interested in knowing more about her.

Technological Preparation

During the interview process, you may need to do different kinds of long-distance interviews, or you may need to prepare presentations. We all know that in these kinds of situations, we may face some unexpected technological errors. The best reaction is to be prepared for any error from your side, and if from another party, you should be patient and understanding about it to avoid creating any embarrassment.

I remember one job-seeker who was sent for an interview with one of our clients and had to do a presentation for them. He showed up for the interview with his laptop and his USB drive, so the PowerPoint presentation was absolutely ready to go. The projector had some kind of problems and didn't work. The good thing was that we had prepared him for this by suggesting he print each slide in colourful copies for each and every interviewer. There were three interviewers to whom he provided a copy of the presentation, and there was no gap in the process at all. When these situations happen due to a snag in technology, and sometimes they may, you can't really control it. Being prepared for the situation with an alternative will save you as well as your interviewers from embarrassment, and the flow of the interview can be maintained.

Thank-you Email

Another very important gesture that I highly recommend you to do is to send a thank-you email to the interviewer/s within a maximum of twenty-four hours after your interview. This is not just a simple thank-you letter; it is showing your sense of appreciation for their time, and it provides you an opportunity to demonstrate your understanding of the role. It also enhances your chances of being the right candidate for the role by providing them with another solid reason why they should choose you. If you got the interview through a recruitment agency, it would be better to send this email to your assigned recruiter and to ask them to share it with the hiring managers on your behalf.

There are certain techniques that I always practise in my consultation sessions. So, from techniques of how to do your research, how to prepare yourself, and how to attempt the interview itself, there are certain things to keep in mind regarding techniques and preparation. These techniques are geared towards the superman pose, the ice breaker, the golden time, the positive attitude that you need to keep up all the way during the interview, and the importance of being prepared for your presentation (if you have one) by bringing along your laptop and everything else you may need. Body language, the power of the smile, and various other things are equally important and can be discussed in detail along with various other topics during my consultation sessions, either in the group class or in the private sessions.

To summarise this chapter:

1) Be prepared by doing your research about the company, the organisation's culture, and the interviewers. Be aware of yourself, your achievements, and how you can add value to the organisation. Be prepared by knowing not only where to go, but what you're going to do as well.

2) Go to the interview with a positive attitude, and use certain skills to ensure that you have a successful interview. Be spontaneous, but be so prepared and confident that you can guarantee that your interview will be a success.

3) Don't be afraid of asking relevant questions during the interview. In the end, thank everyone present for their time and make sure to find out how long the selection process may take. Make sure you have the email address of the interviewer/s, and within no more than twenty-four hours, send a thank-you email to them or your recruiter.

Own your interview, let them never forget you, and convince them that they want you and only you to join their organisation.

In the next two chapters, I shall elaborate on the techniques and key actions that can increase your chances of having a successful interview.

Chapter 8

Your Memorable Trademark or Signature

At the end of the day, people won't remember what you said or did, they will remember how you made them feel.

— *Maya Angelou*

I'M SURE THAT during your lifetime you've seen someone who was just impossible to forget. There are always people in group events, in class, or at work, who shine so brightly that they become memorable. What is their secret of being so unforgettable? This quality is what I call your memorable trademark, something which you also have. Surprising, right? You just need to make sure that you don't keep it only to yourself.

But first, let's find out why it's important for you to have your trademark.

Just by being so unforgettable, it increases your chances of being remembered when opportunities come your way. We've been talking about job-searching in this book, so it's important that you are both seen and remembered, although being remembered is more important than being seen.

Nowadays, recruiters, both internal and external, are loaded with different job vacancies. They are constantly meeting with different applicants. For each position, they may initially speak with more than twenty candidates on the phone, or perhaps they may interview more than five or six candidates face-to-face. Think about a situation where there are five candidates and they all have almost the same qualifications and experience as you do. Why should you be selected in that situation? Here is where the key lies: your signature, your trademark, the one thing that makes you unforgettable and makes you stand out among all the other candidates.

The good news is that everyone has their own trademark, but not everyone knows how to use it to become memorable. This is why they start to feel invisible. They start missing opportunities, and in the end, they feel that they cannot stand out.

What you need to do is to be unforgettable. Have your own trademark; find it in a pleasant way. Let people remember you for your good qualities. Create good memories and good feelings for people.

Your trademark should be something powerful and positive, and it should also make people feel good about themselves. Remember that, as much as you shine and you have your own signature, by also trying to find other people's signatures and recognising them, you can make yourself memorable.

Your special quality doesn't need to be very specific or related to your qualification, per se. It is actually more about your personality, your attitude, your sharpness, or your hard-working attitude and willingness to go out of your way to help others. It can be something completely hidden, but don't be shy of your special quality; be proud of it. Find out what your signature is and become the best in that one quality so that you can show off with it. This will make you stand out and be unforgettable.

I remember one job-seeker specifically. When my team members and I got in touch with him, we were so amazed by how professional and unforgettable he was. He was always ready for action; he always said 'yes' to all our requests and always had a positive attitude. This made him so memorable that we knew, even if he wasn't interested in exploring a certain job opportunity, he would make that phone call or conversation worthwhile by referring other job-seekers he felt were more suitable for the role. He made sure that we wouldn't feel that we were bothering him or making the conversation awkward.

I can understand some of you may think being bold and unforgettable is more related to extroverted people. So, what if you're introverted and shy in nature?

Shyness is not a permanent quality or something that stays with you forever. It's not something you were born with, and you may not always be shy in every situation for the rest of your life. You can overcome your shyness by practising. Part of my nature is also shy. I always believed I was born shy and that I could not change it, but I learned techniques over the years to overcome my shyness, and nowadays I even consider myself a very outspoken person.

I would like to start with myself. I was a shy and isolated child with almost no friends. I couldn't make contact with any of my classmates as I was too shy even by the time I reached university. This quality was with me until my early twenties, until one day when one of my friends—to be specific, the only one I had—asked me to do a speech on her behalf, as she was in a difficult situation with her family. I couldn't say no to her. It was a difficult situation, but I didn't want to let her down. So, I started to practise in various ways, like standing in front of a mirror to be able to overcome my shyness and to do well in public speaking. I presented the speech in front of many people. I was stressed and overwhelmed by the crowd, so I started to laugh naturally many times while I was doing the speech; surprisingly, my laugh became my signature. Everyone remembered me even many years after that speech. As a result, I got many requests for public speaking at the university, and even for some events outside the university. That was the turning point in my life, and at that moment I realised what my memorable trademark was. It was always in me, and eventually, by refusing to be shy about it, it became my memorable trademark.

I started to use my laugh as part of my memorable trademark because it's very loud and I'm told it can be contagious. As I start to laugh, everyone else starts to laugh with me, even if they don't know the reason behind it. I use it in the office. I use it in interviews or when I'm meeting clients. I use it in B2B or business. I can honestly say that if you bring up my name in any meeting, it will just remind them of my laugh.

I have workshops which discuss valuable techniques on how to overcome your shyness, and I highly recommend them if you feel that you are shy by nature and it is hampering you in your job-seeking journey. Using these techniques will make you feel more confident about your personal unforgettable qualities, and I guarantee that you won't be shy to show off your trademark anymore.

You may be thinking, 'Some people don't have any such qualities that make them unforgettable'. I believe that everyone has that unique or, what I call, signature quality. However, if you still think that you don't have it, you can perhaps start with thinking about what you like about others, what you think about others' signatures, and what makes certain people in your life memorable. You can start asking them about these qualities, or you can practise being more like them. They will turn into a role model for you. It doesn't have to be only relatives or friends or people in your network; you can find your role model among influencers on social media as well, like some celebrities or some very famous or successful professionals, so you can follow their steps to become memorable like them.

Sometimes I meet with professionals who feel that maybe their signature is not something that people really like. In this case, you need to find out what the downside is of your signature and change it for the better. Your signature can improve; it's not something fixed that you cannot change. So, you can update it or change it over the years. I'm sure that your special quality has changed over the years. When you were a teenager, you had certain qualities, and then in your youth you had certain other qualities, and as you got wiser, your qualities got better. Try to 'update' your special qualities to make them more about who you are right now. In this way, you can also start figuring out how you can help other people feel better about themselves.

To summarise this chapter, I would like to remind you of three important points:

1) Find your signature or find a signature that you like. Become the best you can be at that quality, be it of your personality or your attitude.

2) You can start using or showing off your quality more often. Start reflecting on those qualities of your personality and don't be shy about showing the memorable part of your personality. Don't forget that it's always good to make other people feel good with your signature or with your memorable quality. In this case, you leave your footprints in their heart.

3) Giving credit and recognition to others, even if you have just met them, by finding certain qualities in them and complimenting them will help you to get recognised in return; it is the key to making you remarkable and memorable.

Chapter 9

Your Master Key

Are you familiar with the phrase 'the master key'? It's actually the key that can open all the doors of a place. What does it have to do with your job-finding process? Let's say that, with the help of all the previous steps, you have gotten to the stage where you have finally gotten an interview. This is action time; this is about how you represent yourself and your master key. How can your master key open up all these possibilities for you? There are tons of techniques on the Internet and in different books about the dos and don'ts of interviews, and I'm sure you know at least the basics by now. But what these sources don't share is that there are some personality traits that can help you to handle the interview in your own way. All you need to do is just own it. The interview is the scene, and you can be yourself and use your master key to open the door to that opportunity.

Why is this important? The interviewers interview many people on a daily basis, and they could get really bored by the clichéd answers they keep hearing. But, as soon as you act differently, they begin to notice that you're not a robot. You will stand out as someone who thinks outside the box, and they immediately feel the difference in your method. You tend to gain a lot of credibility, and it will help you a lot to just differentiate yourself from the rest who are performing an extremely robotic interview.

When job-seekers don't stand out, they miss the chance to get enough recognition, and they can't represent themselves in the best way. This is how they often end up not finding the ideal job.

What is your secret, your master key? It is knowing that 'No one is you and that is your power'. So, ultimately, it is all about you being ready and prepared by understanding the interviewer's needs and showing that you have the ability to fulfil those needs. It is all about you being prepared to show them who you are and to demonstrate that aptly in regard to their needs. To reach that match, you first need to do research not only about them but also about yourself.

Nowadays, the Internet is a good place to carry out your research process. Perhaps you can find out about some volunteer work they have done or some interest that they have shared on their LinkedIn profile so you can demonstrate something that you have in common with them during the interview (without indicating that you've already checked their profile). As a result, you have already built that rapport with them and they will start to feel closer to you. Alternatively, this can help you to break down the wall between you and them very easily. But you need to bear in mind that you won't just have all it takes to allow you to use your master key successfully.

This is the part where you need to think outside the box. You need to go out of your comfort zone. You can maybe even start by getting some insider information. There is some important information to be aware of prior to your interview, such as the culture of the organisation. Some organisations have a very quick way of approaching things, while some are more laid back; that is, they use the 'family' style.

Mirroring

Mirroring is a very powerful technique that you can use in your interview. After you find out about the personality of the interviewer, make sure that you demonstrate the personality quality in you that matches or 'mirrors' this and that you believe the interviewers will really like. For example, if the interviewer is sharp and is looking for a quick answer, make sure you are quick too, or the interviewer might get bored. If they are more relaxed, you don't need to be sharp. Try to mirror their personality, because people like to work with like-minded people and who are pursuing the same goals.

Important Note to Take into Consideration

What if these personalities don't match? This is a very important question that you should ask yourself, but you are the only one who has an honest answer. It is all about you, and this is how you can liberate yourself. You get your freedom, you can choose. Don't forget what your very first reason was for wanting to move to another job, and don't forget that you will be spending 30 percent of your day at this job. You are not going to want to leave your job for temporary better pay or to go to another job that won't serve you. It's all in your hands. It's your 'master key', but it doesn't mean that you have to open all doors at any cost. As long as you are clear about who you are and what you want, you will find the right place. We are not practising to be a fake here just to get the job. Remember your reasons.

Even if you are out of work and you are running out of time to get a job just to survive, if you are not sure if that particular job is something you will enjoy, it will be worth waiting for the right opportunity to fulfil your requirements. It is also not fair to your future employer, as they are investing in you and they need you to be able to fulfil their needs.

I was once in a similar situation myself. I left the market for personal reasons, and I was ready to take up any opportunity that came my way. After one of my interviews, I felt that something was wrong. I didn't see myself performing at my best in the role I had interviewed for, and it had nothing to do with my abilities. It had more to do with the culture of the organisation. For me, a work–life balance was one of the keys that my new role needed to offer, and this was something I didn't see in this opportunity. They asked me how I would feel working long hours, and while I personally don't mind staying behind on one or two occasions to get a project done, if this was the general culture of the company—that I would have to stay on to take on the next day's responsibilities even after I had completed the tasks of the day—that wasn't something I wanted to do. So, in spite of my desperation to find a job, I let go of that opportunity and guess what? Within a week, I found another opportunity that was suitable for me in all aspects.

So, I am sure that you have come to realise that having a 'master key' allows this process to be all about you: who you truly are and what you truly want. You should match your needs to the requirements of the opportunity.

To summarise this chapter, here are three important points that I would like to share with you:

1) Do your research, but don't count solely on an Internet search. Think outside the box. Do some internal search

through your network to understand the culture of the organisation and the interviewer/s.

2) Use the mirroring technique to build a strong rapport with the interviewer and create a pleasant interview flow.

3) Be honest with yourself and your future employer. Don't use your master key to open all doors. Your personality should be a match with that of your co-workers and future organisation. You are going to be a part of them, and you will need to add value to them.

Chapter 10

Final Move Congratulations

After all these stages that you have passed successfully, you have reached the offer stage. This is the final stage and is still extremely important as it could be a deal-breaker. However, if you were prepared earlier and have already covered this part in your interviews, please allow me to say congratulations. You have secured this new opportunity, and it is now time to take care of your resignation from your current organisation.

To have a smooth joining process, make sure

1) You have discussed your salary with someone from the human resources department at the end of the process or in your final interview. Have a list of 'whys' and the values that you can add to the organisation ready for the salary negotiation. Negotiation skill is a soft skill, and it can be learnt through practice. If you feel you need to practise more, sign up for a negotiation consultation and we can go through your specific case. Situations and solution techniques differ from case to case, so by doing this, we can guarantee that you will have a successful negotiation and achieve your targeted package.

2) While you are going through the offer letter, make sure that you read it thoroughly, and if there are parts you are unsure of, contact the relevant person and ask for clarification. While you are performing this step, check in with your reasons, your 'whys'. Sometimes, the salary itself is not your target but the whole package is the aim of moving to a new role. But, within the process, you may have forgotten your initial reasons for looking for other opportunities in the first place.

3) Make sure you understand the whole process and that you have the required documents. Also, be very transparent with your notice period for your current organisation and your timeline for your new organisation. Prepare yourself to hand in your resignation and manage the counter-offer situation.

Congratulations on achieving your goal! What you've learnt through this book is a complete blueprint for searching for a suitable job. It will help you at any stage and will also help you during your future job-hunting process.

If you benefitted from this book at any stage of your search, it would be great if you could share it with your network and increase their chances of having a successful job search as well. It could even become a part of your superhero personality!

This book is a general guideline for a modern job search. If you would like to go one step further and understand your talents so you can find the right career for yourself, I have good news to share with you. You can find these tips in my next book which will be coming out soon. But, if you cannot wait until my next book is released, I do conduct private career-coaching sessions for individuals in search of their true potential and who are looking for their perfect career.

Public Workshops

BY READING THIS book, you are already provided with a basic and sufficient level of information regarding how to progress a career successfully. If you are looking to explore each chapter more deeply, Pegah is also offering public workshops in order to make this process easier. With a little investment, one can attend these workshops and benefit substantially by learning the methods thoroughly and practising the blueprint of every step of the preparation process and action of finding the most suitable job and means of career progression.

Some of the workshops are listed below:

* <u>Preparation</u>

> *By failing to prepare, you are preparing to fail.*

> *—Benjamin Franklin*

✓ **Identify Your Talents and Strengths**
At the end of this workshop, by performing some practical exercises, you will become aware of your **hidden talents and strengths**. You would also be able to use these

hidden talents and strengths in your current role or for future opportunities.

✓ **CV Writing (Write your own CV)**

Your CV is the most important tool in your career. Pegah is a big fan of writing one's own CV and avoiding giving it to third parties (because doing so can result in a cold and repetitive CV).

In this workshop, you will learn the blueprint and be able to use it any time, even years from now. Attending this workshop is a necessity for your career progression.

✓ **Job Search Secrets**

There are many secrets involved when seeking a job, and Pegah has shared them in this book. In this workshop, you will have the opportunity to go in depth, ask questions, and also, gather some ideas from the attendees.

✓ **Be a Superhero**

This is one of the **most popular workshops** offered in any area of career progression, and it is beneficial for all levels (even if you are not job-searching), particularly for improving your methods of communication at a different level, building rapport with others, and creating effective networks.

Highly recommended workshop to attend:

- <u>Action</u>

  Action is the real measure of intelligence.

  — *Napoleon Hill*

✓ **Become a Master in any Interview**
In this interactive workshop, Pegah will practise some role plays and **interview preparation and techniques** with the audience to work on them practically and create a real-life interview scenario.

✓ **Your Trademark**
Become unforgettable. In this workshop, you will enable your master key and your unique trademark to use in all areas of career progression.

By attending any of the above public workshops, you will have the chance to exchange information, share your knowledge, and use this **great opportunity to grow your network**.
For more information on the public workshops,
visit: www.pegahgol.com

About the Author

Pegah Gol is the director of a human resources consulting company, based in the United Arab Emirates, and also a licensed career coach at Career Counselling Services, London. Throughout her career in different executive search firms, she has taken up various roles, such as an in–house HR executive and a director. She thoroughly understands the recruitment process and the right steps needed to be taken for finding a suitable job in the United Arab Emirates, all of which have helped her become a career coach.

In 2004, Pegah has found her passion for human resources, specifically in recruitment. Ever since, she has been coaching and guiding people climb up their career ladder. In her 15 years of experience, Pegah has helped people (from graduates to senior C-level executives), predominantly in the Middle East, take the next big step towards their career growth.

Her philosophy is to guide every individual identify their talents and strengths, and not settle for any job unless they enjoy what they do and are passionate about it. Therefore, with her interest in guiding people to reach their career goals combined with her in-depth knowledge of the modern job-seeking process, she has gathered the fundamental techniques, from A to Z of job finding and career progression and put them together in her book, *The Formula*.

Pegah also conducts public workshops and private coaching sessions, where she emphasizes on identifying the uniqueness of individuals and tailor the coaching accordingly, to help them land best-suited roles in the industry of their choice, and keep them within their expertise.

CPSIA information can be obtained
at www.ICGtesting.com
Printed in the USA
BVHW050109020822
643541BV00011B/1449

9 780648 505020